BREAKING THE STIGMA OF MENTAL HEALTH

Breaking Chains and Dismantling Mental Health Stereotypes

DR. Williams Dosh

ISBN: 9798325549427
Imprint: Independently published

Cover design by: Art Painter Librar Congress Control Number: 2018675309

Printed in the United States of America

DEDICATION

To all those who've dared to share their stories, and to those who've yet to find their voice, May this book serve as a beacon of solidarity, a reminder that in our vulnerability lays our strength. Here's to breaking the chains of stigma together, and to a future filled with compassion, understanding, and unyielding hope.

Table of Contents

INTRODUCTION

The Stigma OF MENTAL HEALTH.
Mental health is an issue that affects millions of people worldwide. Despite its prevalence, there is still a stigma surrounding mental health, which prevents many people from seeking the help they need. The intersection of mental health and identity is a complex issue that requires a nuanced understanding of both. In this part of this book, we explore the ways in which mental health and identity intersect, and how we can work to break the stigma surrounding mental health.

CHAPTER 1

The intersection of mental health and identity
Identity plays an important role in how we perceive ourselves and how others perceive us. Our identity can be shaped by a variety of factors, including our race, gender, sexuality, religion and cultural background. Mental health can also impact our identity, as it can influence our mood, behavior, and overall sense of self. The intersection of mental health and identity is complex, and it is important to recognize the ways in which these two issues are linked.

Breaking the stigma

One of the biggest barriers to seeking mental health treatment is the stigma surrounding mental illness. The stigma can be particularly strong for individuals from marginalized communities, such as people of color or members of the LGBTQ+ community. Breaking the stigma requires a collective effort from all of us, including mental health professionals, policy makers and society at large. Education is the key to breaking the stigma, and it is important to provide accurate information about mental health and the different treatment options available.

The importance of culturally competent care

Culturally competent care is an essential part of mental health care. Culturally competent care means that mental health professionals can provide care that takes into account the cultural and linguistic needs of their clients. This also includes understanding the unique challenges that people from different cultures may face when seeking treatment in mental health care. Culturally competent care can help remove barriers to treatment and ensure that all individuals have access to the care they need.

The role of intersectionality

Intersectionality is a concept that recognizes the ways in which different aspects of our identity intersect and influence our experiences. For example, a person who is both a person of color and a member of the LGBTQ+ community may face unique challenges when seeking mental health treatment. Understanding the role of intersectionality is essential to providing effective mental health care to all individuals.

The need for advocacy

Advocacy is an essential part of breaking the stigma around mental health. Advocacy can take many forms, including educating others about mental health, speaking out against stigma and discrimination, and advocating for policies that promote mental health. Advocacy can also involve sharing personal stories and experiences to help others understand the impact of mental illness .

Overall, the intersection of mental health and identity is a complex issue that requires a nuanced understanding of both. Breaking the stigma around mental health care is essential to ensuring that all individuals have access to the care they need. By providing culturally competent care, understanding the role of intersectionality, and engaging in advocacy, we can work to create a more inclusive and supportive society for people with mental illness.

CHAPTER 2

Civility is an essential communication element that promotes respect and mutual understanding among individuals. In today's fast-paced world, where people are often quick to judge and dismiss others, civility plays a crucial role in maintaining mental health and well-being . Civility promotes an environment of trust and respect, which allow individuals to feel safe and comfortable expressing their thoughts and feelings. Conversely, inadequacy can lead to feelings of isolation, anxiety and depression. The impact of civility on mental health and well-being is significant and far-reaching, affecting individuals, families, communities and affects society as a whole.

Here are some insights into the impact of civility on mental health and well-being:

Civility promotes a sense of belonging:

When individuals feel respected and valued, they are more likely to feel a sense of belonging and connection with others. This sense of belonging is crucial to maintaining mental health and well-being because it reduces feelings of loneliness and isolation.

Infertility Leads to Stress:

Negative interactions, such as name-calling, belittling, and disrespect, can lead to increased stress levels. Chronic stress can have a significant impact on mental health , leading to anxiety, depression, and other mental health conditions .

Civility Encourages Empathy:

When individuals communicate with civility, they are more likely to listen to others and consider their perspectives. This promotes empathy and compassion, which are essential for building strong relationships and maintaining mental health and well-being.

Infertility leads to aggression:

When individuals interact with infertility, it can lead to aggression and conflict. This can have a significant impact on mental health, leading to feelings of anger, frustration and helplessness.

Politeness promotes positive self-talk:

When individuals communicate with politeness, they are more likely to use positive self-talk. Positive self-talk is associated with better mental health care outcomes, including reduced stress and improved well-being.

Civility plays a crucial role in maintaining mental health and well-being. By promoting an environment of respect and understanding, individuals can reduce stress levels, promote empathy and **build strong relationships with others**. Conversely, infertility can have a significant impact on mental health, leading to feelings of isolation, anxiety and depression. It is essential to prioritize civility in our interactions with others to **promote mental health and wellbeing for all**.

CHAPTER 3

Startups and entrepreneurs have access to a range of resources to promote mental wellbeing. Here are some valuable resources to consider:

Employee Assistance Programs (EAPs): EAPs are workplace programs that provide a variety of services to support the mental well-being of employees . These services may include counseling, therapy, and referrals to mental health care professionals. Startups can partner with EAP providers to offer these programs to their teams.

Mental health apps:

There are numerous mental health apps available that provide tools and resources for dealing with stress, anxiety, and other mental health issues. Examples include Headspace, Calm and Mood path. Startups can support and encourage the use of these apps to support the mental well-being of their team members.

Online communities in mental health care:

Online communities provide a platform for individuals to connect, share experiences and seek support. Startups can encourage their teams to join online mental
health communities, such as forums, social media groups, or online support groups.

Mental Health Workshops and Webinars:

Startups can host mental health workshops and webinars to educate their teams on mental health and wellness. These workshops can cover topics such as stress management, building resilience and mindfulness. By providing access to knowledge and skills, startups empower their teams to take charge of their mental well-being.

Mental Health Help lines:

Mental health help lines provide immediate support to individuals in crisis. Startups can provide information
and promote the use of hotlines such as the National Suicide Prevention Lifeline or local crisis hotlines . By making helpline information readily available, startups ensure that their team members have access to immediate help when needed.

Mental health training programs :

Startups can invest in mental health training programs for their managers and leaders. These programs provide skills and knowledge to recognize and address mental health issues in the workplace. By training their leaders, startups create an environment where mental health is prioritized and supported.

By utilizing these resources, startups and entrepreneurs can promote mental well-being within their teams. Investing in the mental health of team members not only supports their well-being, but also contributes to the long-term success and sustainability of startups.

The reality is that unless you understand the regulatory environment and payment structure, you can't revolutionize it. I think most tech companies and startups have come to this realization: that you have to partner with people in the ecosystem.

CHAPTER 4

Having a physical disability can be a challenging experience, but when combined with mental health issues, it can become even more intimidating. The stigma attached to mental health can make it difficult for individuals to seek help, and the added pressure of dealing with a physical disability can worsen symptoms. Coping with these challenges can be a long and difficult journey, but with the right support it is possible to manage both mental and physical health.

Seek Professional Help:

One of the most important steps in dealing with mental health and physical disabilities is seeking professional help. A mental health professional can provide support and guidance to manage symptoms and develop coping strategies. Similarly, a physiotherapist can assist with rehabilitation and provide advice on how to deal with physical limitations. It is important to find professionals who have knowledge of both mental health and physical disabilities to ensure that all aspects of your health are addressed.

Build a Support System:

Having a strong support system is essential when dealing with mental health and physical disabilities. Family, friends, and support groups can create a sense of community and help alleviate feelings of isolation. It is important to communicate your needs and limitations to those around you and to ask for help when needed. Additionally, connecting with others who have similar experiences can provide a sense of understanding and validation.

Practice self-care:

Self-care is an important aspect of managing both mental and physical health. This may include engaging in activities that bring joy and relaxation, such as reading, listening to music, or practicing meditation. It is also important to prioritize physical health by eating healthy, getting enough sleep, and exercising regularly. Taking good care of yourself can help reduce stress and improve overall well-being.

Addressing Stigma:

The stigma surrounding mental health can make it difficult for individuals to seek help and can exacerbate feelings of shame and isolation. Addressing this stigma may include educating oneself and others about mental health, challenging negative attitudes and beliefs, and advocating for mental health resources and support . It's important to remember that mental health problems are common and treatable, and that seeking help is a sign of strength.

Develop coping strategies:

Coping with mental health and physical limitations can involve developing strategies to manage symptoms and challenges. These may include mindfulness techniques, journal writing, and relaxation exercises. It is important to identify triggers and develop a plan for managing them . Developing coping strategies can help individuals gain more control over their health and reduce feelings of helplessness.

Coping with mental health and physical disabilities can be a challenging experience, but with the right support and resources, it is possible to manage both aspects of one's health. Seeking professional help, building a support system, practicing self-care, addressing stigma, and developing coping strategies are all important steps in managing mental and physical health. With patience, perseverance, and a willingness to seek help, individuals can learn to cope with the challenges of living with a physical disability and maintain good mental health.

CHAPTER 5

A Promising Future for Mental Health Startups.

Increased Accessibility and Convenience:

Health's startups have revolutionized the way individual's access and receive mental health care. Traditional therapy often requires individuals to schedule appointments in advance, travel to a physical location, and pay hefty fees. However, with the rise of mental health startups, therapy and support are just a few clicks away. For example, platforms such as TalkSpace and BetterHelp offer virtual therapy sessions that can be conducted from the comfort of one's own home. This increased accessibility and convenience has benefited individuals made it easier to seek help and get the support they need, especially for those who may have limited mobility or live in remote areas without access to mental health care.

Customized and Personalized Care:

Mental health startups are also leveraging technology to provide personalized and tailored care to individuals. Through the use of algorithms and machine learning, these startups are able to analyze data and provide personalized treatment plans based on a person's specific needs. For example, Woebot, an AI-powered chatbot for mental health care, uses natural language processing to provide personalized support and cognitive behavioral therapy techniques to users. By delivering personalized care, they care for mental health Ensure that individuals receive treatment that is most appropriate for their unique circumstances, increasing the likelihood of positive outcomes .

Breaking Stigma and Normalizing Mental Health :

One of the most promising aspects of mental health startups is their ability to break the barriers and stigma associated with seeking help for mental health issues. Many people hesitate to seek therapy or support due to the fear of being judged or stigmatized. However, these startups are working to normalize mental health and make it a topic that can be discussed openly. For example, startups like 7 Cups offer online peer support and anonymous chat rooms where individuals can connect with others who may be experiencing similar challenges. By fostering a sense of community and creating safe spaces for open dialogue, mental health startups are helping reduce the stigma surrounding mental health and encouraging more people to seek the support they need.

Integration of Holistic Approaches:

Mental health startups embrace holistic approaches to mental wellness, recognizing that mental health is not just about therapy or medication, but encompasses various aspects of a person's life. These startups integrate techniques such as mindfulness, meditation and yoga into their platforms to promote overall mental well-being. For example, the startup Headspace offers guided meditation and mindfulness exercises to help individuals reduce stress and improve their mental resilience. By taking a holistic approach, couples are starting mental health care empowering individuals to take charge of their mental health and explore different avenues for self-care and healing.

In conclusion, the future looks promising for mental health startups. With increased accessibility, personalized care, stigma reduction and integration of holistic approaches, these startups are changing lives and transforming the way mental health support is provided. As technology advances and As society becomes more open to discussing mental health, we can expect mental health startups to play an important role in improving mental well-being on a global scale.

CHAPTER 6

Promoting emotional well-being and mental health in schools:

Promoting emotional well-being and mental health in schools is critical to creating safe learning environments. When students feel supported and emotionally stable, they are more likely to participate in their education and achieve academic success. Here are some strategies and tips for promoting emotional well-being and mental health in schools:

Implementing social-emotional learning (SEL) programs:

SEL programs provide students with the necessary skills to manage their emotions, build positive relationships, and make responsible decisions. These programs can be integrated into the curriculum or delivered through specialized workshops. For example, a school might offer a weekly SEL lesson in which students learn about self-awareness, empathy, and conflict resolution.

Creating a Supportive Environment:

Schools should strive to create a supportive environment where students feel safe to express their emotions and seek help when needed. This can be achieved by promoting positive relationships between students and teachers, encouraging open communication and implementing anti-bullying policies. For example, a school may have designated safe spaces where students can go to talk to a trusted adult or counselor.

Providing Mental Health Resources:

Schools must have access to mental health resources and support services to ensure students get the help they need . This may include on-site counselors, partnerships with local mental health care organizations, or referral programs. For example, a school may have a counselor available that students can talk to regularly, or they may organize workshops on stress management and coping skills.

Educate students and staff:

It is important to educate both students and staff about mental health and wellness. By increasing awareness and understanding, schools can reduce stigma and create a more inclusive environment. For example, a school can invite guest speakers to talk about mental health or organize workshops for staff on how to support students with mental health problems.

Case study: XYZ high school

At XYZ High School, promoting emotional well-being and mental health is a top priority. The school has implemented several initiatives to support their students:

- They have integrated a social-emotional learning program into their curriculum, which regularly includes lessons on emotional management, communication skills and empathy.

- XYZ High School has designated mental health professionals who are available on site for students to talk to. These professionals provide counseling services and support students in developing coping strategies.

- The school regularly organizes mental health awareness campaigns, inviting guest speakers to discuss various topics related to mental health and wellbeing. They also provide resources and information to both students and staff.

- XYZ High School has created a supportive environment by implementing anti-bullying policies and promoting positive relationships among students. They have also established a peer support network where older students mentor and support younger students.

By prioritizing emotional well-being and mental health , XYZ High School has created a safe and nurturing learning environment for their students.

In conclusion, promoting emotional well-being and mental health in schools is essential for creating safe learning environments. By implementing social-emotional learning programs, creating a supportive environment, providing mental health resources, and training students and staff, schools can help students thrive academically and emotionally. The case study of XYZ High School demonstrates the positive impact of these strategies in creating a safe and inclusive learning environment.

CHAPTER 7

Breaking the Stigma:

In our ongoing research into resilience and its multifaceted role in our lives, it is crucial to delve into the topic of mental health. Resilience, often seen as the ability to recover from setbacks, is inextricably linked to our mental well-being. It's not just about getting through life's challenges; it's about how we cope, adapt and ultimately become stronger. This section takes a closer look at the vital connection between resilience and mental health, focusing on how we can collectively break the stigma that often surrounds these topics.

Mental health has been a topic shrouded in stigma for far too long. Although significant progress has been made in recent years, misconceptions and prejudices remain. Breaking this stigma is not just a matter of empathy and understanding, but is crucial for promoting the resilience of individuals and society as a whole.

Let's delve deeper into this topic:

Resilience as a buffer for mental health challenges:

Resilience is not just about recovering from setbacks; it's about preventing mental health problems from taking root. People with higher levels of resilience often experience less stress and anxiety, making them less susceptible to mental health problems. Resilience acts as a protective shield and helps individuals deal effectively with stress and setbacks.

Example: Imagine two people facing a similar job loss. One person, with high resilience, may see it as an opportunity for personal growth, while another, with lower resilience, may fall into depression. Resilience can be a game changer in such situations.

Challenging the stigma

Stigma around mental health can be a major barrier to resilience. When individuals are afraid to seek help or talk openly about their problems, it becomes challenging to develop the coping skills necessary for resilience. Initiatives aimed at challenging and dismantling this stigma is essential for promoting resilience.

Example: Celebrities and public figures who openly discuss their mental health issues can inspire others to do the same.

These conversations help normalize the idea that seeking help is a sign of strength, not weakness.

Resilience training

Resilience can be developed and strengthened. Programs and training aimed at building resilience can enable individuals to better cope with adversity and maintain good mental health. These programs often include strategies such as cognitive behavioral therapy, mindfulness, and stress management techniques.

Example: The U.S. Army has implemented resiliency training programs to help soldiers manage the mental and emotional toll of their duties. These programs have been found to improve overall mental health and reduce the risk of developing post-traumatic stress disorder (PTSD).

Cultural perspectives

It is essential to recognize that perceptions of mental health and resilience vary across cultures. Different societies may have unique ways of understanding and addressing these problems. Building resilience and breaking stigma must be done in a culturally sensitive way .

Example: Some Asian cultures place a strong emphasis on 'saving face', which can deter people from seeking help for mental health issues. Recognizing and respecting these cultural nuances is critical in addressing stigma.

Support systems

Building resilience and breaking the stigma of mental health is not a lonely endeavor. A strong support system, including family, friends and professionals, plays a crucial role in helping individuals cope with their mental health issues.

Example: Someone recovering from an addiction often depends on a support network to stay sober. This support provides encouragement, accountability, and a safety net in times of vulnerability.

Educational initiatives

Education is a powerful tool for change. Schools and workplaces can introduce mental health awareness programs that educate individuals about the importance of resilience and the harmful effects of stigma. The more people know, the more likely they are to contribute to breaking the stigma.

Example: Secondary schools that include mental health care in their curriculum provide young people with the knowledge and skills they need to identify and address mental health issues at an early stage.

Resilience and mental health are intertwined aspects of human well-being. Breaking the stigma around mental health is an essential step in promoting resilience, both on an individual and societal level. By understanding the connections between these two areas and taking practical steps to eliminate misconceptions, we can promote healthier, more resilient communities.

CHAPTER 8

Personalized Solutions: Tailoring Mental Health Support to Individuals.

Understanding the need for personalized mental health care

In recent years, the importance of mental health has received significant recognition. People are becoming more aware of the impact mental wellness has on their overall quality of life. And with the rise of mental health startups, individuals now have access to a wide range resources and support systems to meet their unique needs.

The limitations of one-size-fits-all approaches

Historically, mental health support has often been delivered through a one-size-fits-all approach. However, this approach fails to recognize that each individual's experience with mental health is unique. What works for one person may not work for another. others, and this can lead to suboptimal outcomes and frustration for those seeking help.

Personalized solutions in action

Fortunately, mental health startups have revolutionized the way support is provided by offering personalized solutions to the individual. These startups use technology and data to understand each person's specific needs, preferences, and challenges. By doing this, they can create a more effective and targeted approach to mental health support.

Example 1: AI-powered psychic apps

AI-powered psychic apps, such as Woebot and TalkSpace, are excellent examples of personalized solutions in action. These apps use natural language processing and machine learning algorithms to analyze user input and provide personalized recommendations , coping strategies, and therapeutic interventions.

For example, if a user is expressing feelings of anxiety, the app can suggest breathing exercises or mindfulness techniques to help them manage their symptoms. The app's ability to learn from every interaction allows it to tailor its suggestions adapt and refine over time, ensuring a personalized and evolving support system for the user.

Example 2: virtual reality therapy

Another innovative approach to personalized mental health support is virtual reality (VR) therapy. VR allows individuals to immerse themselves in virtual environments that simulate real-life situations, providing a safe space to confront and work through their fears or traumas. Vanquish.

For example, someone with a fear of flying can undergo VR therapy that gradually exposes them to flight-related scenarios, thereby desensitizing and alleviating their fear. By tailoring the virtual experiences to the individual's specific fears and triggers, VR therapy provides a highly personalized and effective treatment option.

The benefits of personalized mental health care:

Personalized mental health support offers several advantages over traditional approaches. First, it increases the likelihood of positive outcomes by addressing the individual's unique needs and challenges. Second, it empowers individuals to take an active role in their journey in mental health care, promoting a sense of ownership and autonomy. Finally, it reduces the stigma associated with seeking help because personalized solutions create a more comfortable and non-judgmental environment for individuals to express their concerns.

In conclusion, the era of one-time mental health support has come to an end. Thanks to the advancement of mental health startups, individuals now have access to personalized solutions that meet their specific needs. Whether it is AI-powered apps or virtual reality therapy, these innovative approaches have revolutionized mental health care and empowered individuals on their journey to wellness.

CHAPTER 9

Taking Steps to Prioritize Mental Health in the Workplace. In recent years, there has been increasing recognition of the importance of mental health in the workplace. Both employers and employees are realizing that a healthy mind is just as crucial as physical well-being when it comes to overall job satisfaction and productivity. This shift in mindset has led to an increased emphasis on creating a work environment that prioritizes mental health and supports employees on their journey to holistic wellness.

One of the most important steps to prioritizing mental health in the workplace is destigmatizing mental health issues. Traditionally, mental health has been a taboo subject, often swept under the rug or dismissed as a sign of weakness. However, by openly discussing mental health and encouraging conversations around it, organizations can create an environment where employees feel safe and supported. This can be done through awareness campaigns, training programs and providing resources such as access to therapy or counseling services. By normalizing conversations about mental health, employees are more likely to seek help when needed and feel comfortable discussing their challenges with their colleagues and managers.

Another important aspect of prioritizing mental health in the workplace is promoting work-life balance. In today's fast-paced and demanding work environments, it's easy for employees to feel overwhelmed and burned out. Encouraging employees to take regular breaks, use their vacation time, and **maintain a healthy work-life balance** can go a long way toward preventing mental health issues. Organizations can implement policies that support flexible work hours and remote work options, and foster a culture that values personal time and self-care. By recognizing that employees have lives outside of work and creating an environment that recognizes the importance of balance, organizations can help reduce stress and improve overall mental well-being .

Additionally, it is critical to provide adequate support and resources to employees struggling with mental health issues. This can include access to mental health professionals, employee assistance programs and wellness initiatives. For example, some companies have implemented mindfulness programs or meditation rooms to help employees relax and reduce stress during the workday. By investing in mental health resources, organizations demonstrate their commitment to the well-being of their employees and create an environment where individuals feel supported and valued.

To effectively prioritize mental health in the workplace, it is essential to involve employees in the decision-making process. By soliciting their input and feedback, organizations can gain valuable insights into the specific needs and challenges employees face. This can be done through surveys, focus groups or regular check-ins. By actively listening to employees and involving them in the development of mental health care initiatives, organizations can create a workplace that truly meets their needs.

Prioritizing mental health in the workplace is not only the right thing to do; it also makes good business sense. By creating an environment that supports mental well-being, organizations can improve employee satisfaction, productivity and retention. By destigmatizing mental health, promoting work-life balance, providing resources, and involving employees in decision-making, organizations can take important steps toward cultivating a mentally healthy workplace. It's time to move forward and make mental health a top priority in every workplace, ensuring employee well-being and promoting a positive and thriving work environment.

• • •

41

CHAPTER 10

Encouraging Self-Care and Seeking Help.
Negative impact on mental health: encouraging self-care and seeking help

Online dating apps have revolutionized the way people meet and connect. However, with the ease and convenience of swiping right or left comes a mental health impact that is often overlooked. The constant need to present yourself in the best light , the fear of rejection, and the pressure to find a perfect match can all take a toll on an individual's mental health . In this section, we discuss the negative impact of online dating apps on mental health and the importance of self-care and seeking help

The negative impact of online dating apps on mental health

Online dating apps have been linked to a variety of negative mental health consequences, such as anxiety, depression and low self-esteem. Research has shown that excessive use of dating apps can lead to a decrease in self-esteem and a distorted view of self-image. The fear of missing out (FOMO) is another factor that can affect mental health. The constant scrolling through profiles and the pressure to **stay on top of the latest trends** can lead to feelings of inadequacy and anxiety. Additionally, the lack of face-to-face communication can lead to social isolation, which can further exacerbate mental health issues.

The importance of self-care

Self-care is crucial for maintaining good mental health, especially when using online dating apps. Taking breaks from dating apps, setting boundaries, and prioritizing self-care activities like exercise, meditation, and spending time with loved ones can all help reduce stress and anxiety. It is essential to remember that taking care of yourself is not selfish, but rather a necessary step towards maintaining good mental health.

Seek help

Seeking help is also an important part of maintaining good mental health. If you suffer from anxiety, depression, or another mental health problem, it is important to seek professional help. Online therapy or counseling can be a good option for people who may not have access to traditional therapy. It is also important to reach out to loved ones and friends for support and to talk about your feelings.

Comparison with traditional dating

While online dating apps have their drawbacks, traditional dating methods also have their own challenges. Meeting someone through friends, at work or in a social setting can also be stressful and anxiety-provoking. However, traditional dating methods allow for more face-to-face communication, which can help build stronger connections and reduce feelings of social isolation.

Online dating apps have revolutionized the dating scene, but they also come with their own challenges. The negative impact on mental health is often overlooked, and it is essential to prioritize self-care and seek help when needed. Taking breaks from dating apps, setting boundaries, and seeking professional help are all important steps toward maintaining good mental health. While traditional dating methods come with their own challenges, they also allow for more face-to-face communication, which can help build stronger connections. Overall, it's important to find a balance that works for you and to put your mental health above all else.

CHAPTER 11

The impact of disrupted attachment on mental health. Attachment disruption is a term used to describe a situation in which a child or adult experiences a breakdown in the emotional bond with his/her primary caregiver. This can have various causes, such as neglect, abuse or divorce. The impact of attachment disorder on mental health is significant and can manifest in a variety of forms, including anxiety, depression and difficulties establishing and maintaining relationships.

The impact of disrupted attachment on children's mental health:

Disturbed attachment can have profound consequences for a child's mental health. Children who experience disrupted attachment may develop attachment disorders, which can manifest as difficulties establishing and maintaining relationships, trust issues, and emotional dysregulation. Attachment disorders can lead to a range of psychological problems, including anxiety, depression and behavioral problems.

For example, children who experience attachment disruption may have difficulty forming healthy relationships later in life, which can make it difficult for them to build support networks and maintain healthy boundaries. They may also struggle with emotional regulation, leading to outbursts and problems managing stress.

The impact of impaired attachment on adult mental health

Disturbed attachment can also have significant consequences for adult mental health. Adults who experienced attachment disruption as children may struggle with anxiety, depression and problems establishing and maintaining relationships. They may also experience feelings of loneliness and isolation, which can worsen mental health problems.

For example, adults who have experienced attachment disruption may have difficulty forming healthy romantic relationships, which can lead to feelings of loneliness and isolation. They may also struggle with trust issues, making it difficult for them to build support networks and maintain healthy boundaries.

Treatment options for disrupted adhesion

Fortunately, there are several treatment options available for people who have experienced attachment disorders. One effective treatment is attachment-based therapy, which focuses on building healthy attachment bonds between client and therapist. This therapy can help clients learn healthy attachment behaviors and build supportive relationships.

Another treatment option is cognitive behavioral therapy (CBT), which can help clients identify and change negative thought patterns and behaviors that can impact their mental health. CBT can be especially helpful for people struggling with anxiety and depression.

Prevention of disrupted adhesion

Preventing attachment disorders is key to promoting healthy mental health outcomes. One way to prevent disrupted attachment is by promoting a healthy attachment bond between parents and children. This can be achieved through interventions such as parent-child interaction therapy (PCIT), which focuses on improving the quality of parent-child interactions.

Another way to prevent bond disruption is to provide support to families at risk of bonding disorder. This may include providing resources such as counseling, financial assistance, and parenting education.

Disturbed attachment can have significant consequences for mental health. However, effective treatment options are available, and prevention is critical in promoting healthy attachment bonds and preventing attachment disorders. By promoting healthy attachment bonds, we can ensure that individuals have the tools they need to build supportive relationships and maintain healthy mental health outcomes.

CHAPTER 12

The Benefits of an Uninterrupted Focus on Mental Health.
In today's fast-paced world, mental health has become a pressing concern for people of all ages. The stress of work, relationships and other responsibilities can take their toll on a person's mental well-being. Therefore, it is essential to **prioritize mental health** and take steps to maintain it. An uninterrupted focus on mental health can help individuals achieve optimal results in all aspects of their lives. In this part we explore the benefits of an uninterrupted focus on mental health.

Improved emotional well-being:

When individuals focus on their mental health, they experience improved emotional well-being. They become more self-aware and can control their emotions better. This leads to a reduction in stress and anxiety levels, which in turn improves their mood and general well-being.

Improved Productivity:

A healthy mind is essential for productivity. When individuals focus on their mental health , they are more likely to be productive and efficient at their jobs. They can concentrate better, make better decisions and solve problems more effectively.

Increased resilience:

Continuous attention to mental health helps individuals develop resilience. They learn to deal with setbacks and challenges and recover from them. This resilience helps them face and overcome difficult situations with a positive attitude.

Better Relationships:

Mental health plays a crucial role in maintaining healthy relationships. When individuals focus on their mental health , they become better communicators and listeners. They can understand their own emotions and those of others, which leads to better relationships.

Improved physical health:

Mental health and physical health are linked. An uninterrupted focus on mental health can lead to better physical health . When individuals manage their stress and anxiety levels, they experience better sleep patterns , better digestion, and better overall health .

An uninterrupted focus on mental health is crucial to achieving optimal results in all aspects of life. It leads to improved emotional well-being, higher productivity, greater resilience, better relationships and better physical health. Therefore, individuals must prioritize their mental health and take steps to maintain it. This may include seeking professional help, practicing mindfulness, engaging in physical activity and maintaining a healthy lifestyle. By doing this, individuals can live fulfilling lives and achieve their goals with laser-sharp focus.

CHAPTER 13

Problem gambling is a major concern for many countries around the world and **its impact on mental health** cannot be ignored. Many researchers have studied the relationship between problem gambling and mental health and have found that there is a strong correlation between the two. People with a gambling problem are more likely to have mental health problems such as depression, anxiety disorders and substance abuse. The reasons behind the relationship between gambling problems and mental health are complex and multi-faceted, and there are different perspectives on this issue.

Psychological perspective:

This perspective suggests that people who engage in gambling often try to escape negative emotions such as anxiety, depression or stress. Gambling can be seen as a way to cope with these emotions because it provides a temporary escape from reality. However, this temporary relief can lead to addiction, which can negatively impact mental health .

Biological perspective:

This perspective suggests that there may be a biological basis for the relationship between problem gambling and mental health. Some studies have shown that people who engage in gambling have lower levels of serotonin, a neurotransmitter associated with mood regulation. This could explain why people with gambling problems are more likely to suffer from depression and anxiety.

Sociological perspective:

This perspective suggests that the relationship between problem gambling and mental health is influenced by social factors such as poverty, social isolation and lack of support. People living in poverty or socially isolated may use gambling as a way to escape their situation. However, this can lead to addiction and further isolation, which can have a negative effect on mental health .

The impact on families:

Problem gambling affects not only the individual but also their family members. Family members of problem gamblers often suffer from stress, anxiety and depression due to the financial and emotional strain caused by the addiction. This can lead to family rifts and further exacerbate the mental health problems of everyone involved.

Treatment Options:

There are several treatment options available for people with gambling and mental health problems. These include therapy, medication, and support groups. Cognitive behavioral therapy has been shown to be effective in treating both gambling problems and mental health problems. Support groups such as Gamblers Anonymous can also provide a supportive community for individuals struggling with addiction.

Problem gambling and mental health are closely linked, and it is important to address both issues in order to provide effective treatment. By understanding the different perspectives on the relationship between problem gambling and mental health , we can develop strategies to prevent and treat addiction while promoting better mental health for both individuals and families.

CHAPTER 14

The impact of mental health awareness campaigns.
Mental health awareness campaigns have had a significant
impact on society, shedding light on the importance of mental
wellbeing and promoting understanding and support for those
struggling with mental health issues. These campaigns aim to
reduce stigma, increase knowledge and encourage open
conversations about mental health.

From the perspective of individuals with lived experiences,
mental health awareness campaigns have provided a platform
for sharing personal stories and raising awareness about
various mental health issues. By sharing their journeys, these
individuals have helped break down barriers and promote
empathy and understanding among the general public .

On the other hand, mental health professionals and
organizations have deployed awareness campaigns to educate
the public about the signs and symptoms of mental illness,
available resources, and treatment options. These campaigns
have played a crucial role in encouraging early intervention and

* * *

seeking professional help, ultimately leading to better outcomes for people struggling with mental health issues.

To delve deeper into the impact of mental health awareness campaigns, let's explore some key insights :

Greater recognition:

Mental health care campaigns have contributed to greater recognition of mental health as an essential part of overall well-being. They have helped people understand that mental health is just as important as physical health and that seeking support is a sign of strength.

Reduced stigma:

Awareness campaigns have played a crucial role in reducing the stigma surrounding mental health . By challenging stereotypes and misconceptions, these campaigns have encouraged open discussions and created a more supportive environment for individuals struggling with mental health issues.

Improved access to resources:

Mental health awareness campaigns have highlighted the availability of resources such as help lines, support groups and therapy services. This increased awareness has made it easier for individuals to access the help they need and find appropriate support networks .

Empowered Communities:

These campaigns have empowered communities to take action and support mental health goals. They have inspired individuals to become advocates, volunteers and allies, fostering a sense of collective responsibility towards mental health issues.

Policy changes:

Mental health awareness campaigns have also influenced policy changes at various levels. By raising public awareness and generating momentum, these campaigns have pushed for better mental health services, increased funding, and the implementation of supportive policies.

Let's look at an example to illustrate the impact of mental health awareness campaigns. The "Let's Talk" campaign, initiated by a mental health care organization, encouraged individuals to share their experiences with mental health and engage in conversations with friends, family and colleagues. This campaign led to a significant increase in public discussions about mental health, less stigma and a greater willingness to seek help.

Mental health awareness campaigns have had a profound impact on society by promoting understanding, reducing stigma and improving access to resources. Through personal stories, education and community engagement, these campaigns have played a crucial role in supporting mental health issues and promoting a more compassionate and inclusive society.

CHAPTER 15

Understanding Mental Health Marketing.

The business angle:

- **Brand reputation and social responsibility:** Companies recognize that aligning with mental health goals improves their brand reputation. Consumers increasingly expect companies to engage in social responsibility, and supporting mental health initiatives shows a commitment that goes beyond profit margins.

- **Market differentiation:** because marketing distinguishes companies from competitors. When a brand actively supports mental health, it becomes more recognizable and memorable. For example, **Bell Let's Talk** in Canada has become synonymous with mental health awareness thanks to its annual campaign .

- **Employee Engagement:** Companies committed to mental health care promote employee loyalty and engagement.

Initiatives such as **employee assistance programs (EAPs) and** mental health care days contribute to a healthier workforce.

The Nonprofit Perspective:

- **Funding and Awareness:** Nonprofits rely on cause marketing to secure funding. Collaborations with companies expand their reach and increase awareness. For example, **To Write Love on Her Arms (TWLOHA)** worked with clothing brands to promote conversations about mental health.

- **Navigating authenticity:** Nonprofits must carefully choose partners that align with their mission. Authenticity is important; an inappropriate collaboration can damage credibility. For example, **NAMI (National Alliance on Mental Illness)** partners with companies that genuinely cares about mental health.

- **Leverage corporate resources:** Nonprofits benefit from corporate resources: financial support, marketing expertise and access to a broader audience. These partnerships increase their impact.

The role of the consumer:

- **Conscious consumerism:** consumers increasingly support brands that align with their values. Marketing for mental health care empowers consumers to make informed choices.

When they buy products related to mental health care campaigns, they contribute to charity.

- **Demand for transparency:** consumers demand transparency. They examine charities' marketing efforts, looking for authenticity. Brands must be clear about the direct impact of their contributions to mental health initiatives.

- **Strengthening Social Media:** Consumers play a crucial role in spreading awareness. Sharing charity-related content on social media reinforces the message. For example, **#WorldMentalHealthDay** is an annual trend, which stimulates conversations.

Examples of effective marketing for mental health reasons:

- **Dove's Self-Esteem Project:** Dove's campaign focuses on body positivity and self-esteem. By working with mental health care organizations, they promote positive body image and mental well-being.

- **Heads Together (UK):** Heads Together, collaboration between **Prince William, Kate Middleton and Prince Harry**, aims to reduce the stigma surrounding mental health. Their collaboration with brands like **Virgin Money** and **Headspace** has sparked meaningful conversations.

- **Mental Health America (MHA) and Walgreens:** MHA's partnership with Walgreens during **Mental Health Month** encourages screenings and destigmatizes discussions about mental health.

In summary, mental health marketing transcends profit margins – it promotes a collective commitment to wellness. As consumers, workers, and advocates, we have the power to shape this narrative and create a world where mental health is prioritized. Let's continue these conversations and create positive change.

CHAPTER 16

Building the Link between Mental Health and Wealth.

Mental health is a crucial aspect of building wealth because it can greatly influence an individual's financial decisions and overall financial well-being. Studies have even shown that those who struggle with mental health issues are more likely to experience financial difficulties. On the other hand, individuals who **prioritize their mental health** tend to make better financial decisions and are more likely to achieve financial success.

The impact of mental health on financial decisions

Mental health problems such as depression, anxiety, and addiction can lead to impulsive and irrational financial decisions. For example, individuals struggling with depression may overspend on material possessions as a temporary means of feeling better. Those with anxiety may avoid making financial decisions altogether taken, leading to missed opportunities for financial growth. Addiction can also lead to financial problems, as individuals may prioritize their addiction over their financial responsibilities.

The importance of financial education in mental health treatment

Financial education can play a crucial role in treating mental health issues. By learning about personal finance, individuals can gain a sense of control over their financial situation and feel empowered to make better financial decisions.
Financial therapy, which combines traditional therapy with financial education, it can be especially helpful for those struggling with mental health issues.

The benefits of budgeting for mental health

Budgeting can also be a powerful tool for improving mental health. By creating a budget, individuals can gain a sense of control over their finances and reduce financial stress. This can lead to improved mental health and a greater chance of achieving financial goals. Reaches.

The role of support systems in building wealth and mental health

Building a strong support system can be essential for both wealth building and mental health. Support systems can provide emotional support during difficult times, provide accountability for financial goals, and provide guidance and advice on financial decisions. This can be especially important for individuals who struggling with psychological problems.

The connection between self-care and financial success

Self-care is crucial for both mental health and financial success. By prioritizing self-care , individuals can improve their mental health, reduce stress, and increase their productivity and focus. This can lead to better financial decisions and a greater chance of achieving financial goals.

Prioritizing mental health is essential to building wealth and achieving financial success. By addressing mental health issues, financial education, budgeting, building a strong support system, and prioritizing self-care, individuals can improve their financial well-being and improve overall quality of life.

CHAPTER 17

Prioritizing Mental Health and Emotional Well-Being .
The importance of prioritizing mental health and emotional well-being in the workplace cannot be overstated. Employees who struggle with their mental health or emotional well-being are at risk of burnout, decreased productivity and increased absenteeism. Additionally, employees who do not support in these areas are more likely to leave their jobs, contributing to high turnover rates. Recognizing and addressing mental health and emotional well-being in the workplace is essential to promoting a healthy and productive work environment.

One way to **prioritize mental health** and emotional well-being in the workplace is to offer employee assistance programs (EAPs). EAPs provide confidential counseling and support services for employees struggling with personal or work-related issues. These programs can help employees manage stress, anxiety, depression and other mental health issues. By offering EAPs, companies demonstrate their commitment to the well-being of their employees and provide them with the tools they need to overcome personal or professional challenges.

Another way to prioritize mental health and emotional well-being is by promoting work-life balance. Employees who feel overworked or overwhelmed are at risk of burnout, which can lead to reduced productivity and increased absenteeism .Employers can promote work-life balance by offering flexible work arrangements, such as telecommuting, flexible scheduling, or job sharing. These arrangements can help employees manage their workloads while attending to personal responsibilities. By promoting work-life balance and personal lives, companies can create a culture that values the well-being of its employees.

Managers can also play a crucial role in prioritizing mental health and emotional well-being. By promoting open communication and encouraging employees to seek support when needed, managers can create a supportive work environment. Managers can also help employees set **realistic goals and set expectations**, which can reduce stress and promote a sense of accomplishment. Additionally, managers can be trained to recognize signs of burnout or other mental health issues and provide support or referrals to appropriate resources.

Finally, companies can prioritize mental health and emotional well-being by offering wellness programs that promote healthy behaviors. These programs can include activities such as yoga, meditation, or exercise classes. By promoting physical health and well-being, companies can also have a positive impact on mental health and emotional well-being.

Prioritizing mental health and emotional well-being in the workplace is essential to promoting a healthy and productive work environment. By offering EAPs, promoting work-life balance , promoting open communication, and offering wellness programs, companies can demonstrating their commitment to the well-being of their employees and reducing turnover rates. Ultimately, investing in employees' mental health and emotional well-being is a win-win for both employees and employers.

CHAPTER 18

Tackling Mental Health in the Workplace.
The importance of mental health in the workplace

Mental health is an integral part of overall well-being and its impact on workplace productivity cannot be overstated. When employees experience stress, anxiety or other mental health issues, it directly impacts their performance, engagement and job satisfaction. Here are some important points to consider:

- **Productivity and absenteeism** : poor mental health can lead to reduced productivity and increased absenteeism. Employees struggling with mental health issues may find it difficult to concentrate meet deadlines or work effectively with colleagues.

- **Stigma and disclosure**: Despite growing awareness, there is still a stigma associated with mental health. Many employees hesitate to make their problems public for fear of judgment or potential consequences for their careers. Creating a supportive environment where employees feel safe to talk about mental health is critical.

- **Work-life balance**: Employers play an important role in **promoting work-life balance**. Encouraging flexible work arrangements, providing resources for mental health care, and promoting a culture that values wellness contribute to a healthier workforce.

Strategies for addressing mental health

Now let's look at practical strategies for tackling mental health in the workplace:

- **Employee Assistance Programs (EAPs)** :

- EAPs provide confidential counseling services to employees dealing with personal or work-related issues. These programs provide employees with a safe space to discuss their mental health issues and receive professional guidance.

- Example: A marketing manager struggling with anxiety can access an EAP to talk to a counselor about coping strategies.

- **Training and awareness programs**:

- Regular mental health awareness training sessions can educate employees and managers on how to recognize signs of anxiety reduce stigma and promote a supportive atmosphere.

- Example: A workshop on stress management teaches employees practical techniques for dealing with work-related pressure.

- **Flexible working arrangements**:

- Allowing flexible schedules, remote work options or compressed work weeks can relieve stress and improve work-life balance.

- Example: A parent with young children may occasionally work from home to manage family responsibilities.

- **Promote social connections**:

- Encourage team building activities, social events and open communication. Strong social connections reduce feelings of isolation and improve mental well-being .

- Example: A monthly team lunch promotes camaraderie and gives employees the opportunity to connect outside of their work duties.

3. Case Study: XYZ Corporation's Mental Health Care Initiatives

Let's take a look at how XYZ Corporation is successfully addressing mental health:

- **XYZ's Wellbeing Portal**:

- XYZ offers an online wellness portal with resources on stress management, mindfulness and coping strategies. Employees have access to articles, videos and self-assessment tools.

- Example: An engineer dealing with burnout finds useful tips on the portal and learns about stress reduction techniques.

- **Mental health champions:**

- XYZ appoints mental health care champions within each department. These staff members receive training to recognize signs of distress and provide peer support.

- Example: A sales manager notices a team member's disengagement and connects him/her to the Mental Health Care Champion for a confidential discussion.

Prioritizing mental health in the workplace benefits both employees and the organization. By fostering a culture of empathy, providing resources, and implementing targeted strategies, companies can create a healthier, more productive workforce. Keep in mind that addressing mental health is not just a checkbox, but an ongoing commitment to employee well-being.

CHAPTER 19

Promoting a Culture of Acceptance and Support.
In todays fast-paced and competitive work environment, mental health issues are becoming increasingly common. The pressure to perform, meet deadlines and constantly strive for success can negatively impact employees' mental well-being .

However, despite the growing recognition of *mental health* issues, there is still widespread stigma surrounding these conditions. This stigma not only prevents individuals from seeking help, but also perpetuates a culture of silence and shame. It is essential for organizations to break this stigma and promote a culture of acceptance and support, where employees feel comfortable discussing their *mental health* issues without fear of judgment or retaliation.

Breaking the stigma surrounding *mental health* requires a collective effort from all levels of an organization. Leaders play a critical role in setting the tone and creating an inclusive environment where employees feel safe to share their experiences. By openly discussing their own *mental health issues, leaders can show vulnerability and encourage others* to do the same.

This transparency helps humanize the issue and shows that it is not a sign of weakness, but rather a natural part of *the human experience.*

Promote education and awareness:

Providing employees with *mental health* education and resources can help dispel misconceptions and increase understanding. This can be done through workshops, training or even informative newsletters. By equipping employees with knowledge, they can better support their colleagues and recognize when someone needs help.

Implement supportive policies and practices:

Organizations should prioritize mental health by implementing policies that support employee well-being. This may include flexible working arrangements, mental health days or access to counseling services. Prioritizing *mental health* in the workplace helps employees feel valued and supported, reducing the stigma associated with seeking help.

Foster a culture of empathy and support:

Encouraging open conversations about mental health and providing a supportive environment can make a significant difference in breaking down stigma. Managers and colleagues should be trained to respond empathetically and nonjudgmentally when someone shares his or her problems. This can be as simple as *actively listening* , offering support and connecting them to *the right resources* .

Lead by example:

Leaders must model behaviors that promote a culture of acceptance and support. This can include taking breaks, prioritizing self-care, and encouraging a healthy work-life balance . When employees see that their leaders value *mental health* and wellness, they are more likely to feel comfortable doing the same.

Provide access to resources:

Organizations should ensure employees have access to mental health resources and support networks. This may include employee support programs, counseling services, or partnerships with mental health organizations. By making these **resources available**, employees are more likely to seek help and feel supported on their journey to *mental wellness.*

Celebrate diversity and individuality:

Recognize that everyone's mental health journey is unique and there is no **one-size-fits-all** solution. Embrace diversity and encourage employees to share their experiences and coping mechanisms. By celebrating individuality, organizations can create a sense of belonging and acceptance, fostering a culture where *mental health* is valued and supported.

Breaking the stigma surrounding mental health in the workplace is an ongoing process that requires commitment and effort from all stakeholders. By promoting education, implementing supportive policies, promoting empathy, leading by example, providing resources, and celebrating individuality, organizations can create a culture of acceptance and support. By doing this, they not only improve employee well-being, but also improve productivity, creativity and *the overall success* of the organization.

CHAPTER 20

Understanding the connection between mental health and finances.

When we think about our finances, we often focus on the numbers: how much money we have, how much we owe, and how we can make more. However, it is important to recognize that our financial well-being is closely linked to our mental health. Financial stress can lead to anxiety, depression and other mental health issues, while poor mental health can make it harder to manage our finances effectively. In this section we explore the connection between *mental health* and finances, and how *financial coaching* and therapy can help.

The connection between *mental health* and finances

Research has shown that there is a strong link between *mental health* and finances. Financial stress can cause anxiety and depression, but can also lead to physical health problems such as headaches and high blood pressure. On the other hand, *mental health* issues can make it more difficult to manage finances effectively, leading to *financial problems* and stress.

The role of *financial coaching*

Financial coaching can be a valuable tool for people struggling with their finances and mental health. A financial coach can help clients set financial goals, create a budget and develop a plan to pay off debt. Additionally, a financial coach can provide emotional support and motivation, helping clients stay on track and avoid the stress that comes with *financial problems*.

The benefits of therapy

Therapy can also be a helpful tool for people struggling with both mental and *financial problems*. Therapy can help clients manage stress, anxiety, and depression, which in turn can make it easier to manage their finances effectively. Additionally, therapy can help clients identify and address the underlying issues that may be contributing to their *financial problems*.

The importance of self-care

Self-care is an important aspect of both *mental health* and *financial well-being*. Taking care of *our physical and emotional health* can help us manage stress and anxiety, while also giving us the energy and motivation we need to stay on track with our finances. Self-care can include things like exercise, meditation, spending time with loved ones, and engaging in hobbies and activities that bring us joy.

Seek professional help

For people struggling with both mental and financial problems, seeking professional help is often the best option. A financial coach or therapist can provide the support and guidance needed to effectively manage both aspects of *a person's life*. In addition, seeking help early can prevent problems from becoming more serious and difficult to manage.

It is important to recognize the connection between *mental health* and finances. Financial stress can contribute to *mental health* problems, while poor *mental health* can make it more difficult to manage finances effectively. Seeking professional help, whether through *financial coaching* or therapy, can be a valuable resource for people struggling with both aspects of their lives. With *the right support* and guidance, it is possible to achieve both financial and mental well-being.

CHAPTER 21

Promoting Mental Health Awareness through Blogging. Sharing personal experiences and stories through blogging has become an effective tool for breaking the stigma surrounding mental health. By openly discussing our struggles, fears and triumphs, we can create a safe and supportive space for others to do the same do. Through the power of words, bloggers play a crucial role in promoting mental health awareness and encouraging conversations that were once considered taboo.

1. Blogging allows individuals to share their unique perspectives on *mental health*, providing a platform for different voices to be heard. For example, someone who has battled anxiety for years can share their coping mechanisms and self-care strategies and provide comfort and guidance to those who may be going through a similar experience. By presenting the realities of living with *mental illness, bloggers dispel misconceptions and promote empathy among their readers.*

2. Additionally, blogging serves as a source of validation and support for people struggling with mental health issues. When individuals read about others who have faced similar challenges and emerged stronger, it instills hope and inspires them to seek help or make positive changes in to their lives. Bloggers who openly discuss their therapy journeys, medication management, or other treatment options can empower their readers to take control of *their mental well-being.*

3. Another important aspect of *mental health* blogging is providing education and resources. Many bloggers dedicate sections of their blogs to sharing valuable information about mental health disorders, symptoms, and available support systems. By doing this, they contribute to breaking the barriers of ignorance and misinformation about *mental health*, ultimately encouraging individuals to seek *professional help* when needed.

4. The anonymity of blogging also allows individuals to share their deepest emotions and thoughts in a safe and non-judgmental environment. This can be particularly helpful for people who find it difficult to express themselves face-to-face or fearing the consequences of disclosing their *mental health* struggles. Through their writing, bloggers create a connection with their readers and remind them that they are not alone in their experiences.

5. The power of storytelling is undeniable and blogging provides an avenue for individuals to create stories that challenge societal norms and perceptions about mental health. By sharing personal stories of resilience, recovery and personal growth , bloggers can narrative around *mental health* , ultimately reducing the stigma associated with it. These stories can act as a catalyst for change, encouraging society to see *mental health* as an integral part of *public well-being*.

6. Finally, blogging for *mental health* not only benefits readers, but also provides *a therapeutic outlet* for the bloggers themselves. Writing can serve as a form of self-reflection, allowing individuals to process their emotions and experiences. By openly sharing their own journey, bloggers often find a sense of catharsis and healing, while also inspiring others to embark on their own paths of self-discovery and growth.

By blogging, individuals are breaking the silence and promoting a sense of community around mental health. By sharing personal experiences, providing education and challenging societal norms, bloggers have a significant impact on promoting mental *health* awareness and breaking the stigma associated with it.

CHAPTER 22

Empowering employees to prioritize their well-being and mental health .

The importance of prioritizing employee well-being and mental health cannot be overstated. Employees who feel supported and valued are more likely to be productive and engaged in the workplace. Furthermore, an organization that prioritizes the well-being of its employees, more likely to attract and retain top talent. However, despite the importance of employee well-being, many organizations do not prioritize it. A study by the *American Psychological* Association found that only 44% of employees believe that their employer well-being. This can have *serious consequences* for employee morale, engagement and productivity.

To tackle this problem, organizations must empower their employees **to prioritize their own wellbeing and mental health.** Here are *some ways* organizations can do this:

1. Provide resources: Organizations should provide employees with access to resources that can help them manage their mental health and well-being. This can include access to

counseling services, *mental health* hotlines, and employee assistance programs.

2. Create a culture of support: Organizations need to create a culture that supports employee wellbeing and mental health. This can include promoting work- life balance, encouraging employees to take breaks and recharge and provide opportunities for employees to connect with each other.

3. Leading by Example: Leaders within the organization must prioritize their own well-being and *mental health*. This may include taking breaks, using their vacation time, and modeling *healthy work habits*.

4. Encourage communication: Organizations should encourage employees to communicate openly about their mental health and well-being. This may include providing training on how to have difficult conversations, creating safe spaces for employees to share their experiences and promote a culture of empathy and understanding.

By empowering employees to prioritize their own well-being and mental health, organizations can create a more engaged and productive workforce. Additionally, by demonstrating a commitment to employee well-being, organizations can attract and retain top talent.

CHAPTER 23

Long-term commitment to mental health initiatives. *Mental health* awareness and advocacy have gained significant momentum in recent years. Organizations, businesses and individuals recognize the importance of tackling mental health issues and promoting wellbeing. However, short-term campaigns and one-off initiatives are not enough to achieve lasting change. To truly support *mental health care*, a long-term commitment is essential. In this section, we explore various aspects of sustaining *mental health* initiatives over time, drawing insights from different perspectives.

Corporate Responsibility and Sustainability:

- Companies play a unique role in advancing mental health care. In addition to occasional awareness campaigns, companies can integrate mental health into their core values and activities. For example:

- **Employee wellness programs:** Organizations can offer comprehensive wellness programs, including *mental health* support. This may include access to counseling services, stress management workshops and *flexible working arrangements.*

- **Leadership buy-in:** When leaders **prioritize mental health**, it sends a powerful message. Leaders can champion mental health initiatives, allocate resources, and create a supportive work environment.

- **Supplier and customer engagement:** Companies can increase their engagement by working with suppliers and customers who share their values. For example, by purchasing products from socially responsible suppliers or collaborating with non-profit organizations in the field of *mental health.*

Community-based approaches:

- *Sustainable mental health* initiatives often start at the community level. Grassroots organizations, *local governments* and community centers play *a crucial role:*

- **Peer Support Networks:** These networks provide *emotional support,* information and coping strategies. They promote a sense of belonging and reduce isolation.

- **Community events:** Regular events such as *mental health* walks, workshops and art exhibitions keep the conversation alive. They also raise money for ongoing programs.

- **School programs:** Educating young people about mental health creates a foundation for lifelong awareness. Schools can integrate *mental health* education into their curricula.

Research and evidence-based practices:

- *Long-term engagement requires* evidence-based approaches. Research informs *effective strategies*:

- **Longitudinal studies:** Tracking mental health outcomes over time helps identify trends and evaluate interventions. Researchers can assess the impact of prevention programs, *early interventions*, and efforts to reduce stigma.

- **Collaboration with academia:** partnerships with universities and research institutions improve knowledge exchange. Researchers can study the effectiveness of different interventions and adjust them based on findings.

- **Continuous learning:** Mental health professionals must stay abreast of best practices . Conferences, webinars and peer-reviewed journals contribute to continuous learning.

Policy advocacy and legislative changes:

- Sustainable impact often requires *systemic changes*. Advocacy efforts can influence policy and laws:

- **Lobbying for Mental Health Legislation: Advocacy groups work tirelessly to** improve mental health policy. Examples include parity laws (equal insurance coverage for *mental health care*) and anti-discrimination measures.

- **Promoting *mental health* policies in the workplace:** Encouraging employers to implement *mental health policies, such as paid mental health* days and reasonable accommodations, will create *lasting change.*

- *Public awareness campaigns*: Advocacy campaigns increase public awareness and build support for policy changes. They encourage citizens to engage with *elected officials.*

Collaboration and partnerships:

- No entity can address mental health challenges alone. Collaboration is essential:

- **Cross-sector partnerships:** Businesses, nonprofits, government agencies and academia can work together. *Joint initiatives* increase impact and pool resources.

- **Global Networks:** International partnerships share best practices and tackle *mental health* on *a global scale.* Organizations such as the World Health Organization (WHO) promote learning between countries.

- **Engage celebrities and influencers:** High-profile individuals can use their platforms to advocate for mental health. Their long-term commitment increases awareness and reduces stigma.

Example: The 'Bell Let's Talk' campaign in Canada is an example of a long-term commitment. Bell, a telecommunications company, started this initiative in 2010. Each year they allocate money to mental health programs based on social media interactions (using the hashtag #BellLetsTalk). The campaign has become an annual event, sparking conversations and funding *essential services.*

In summary, a sustainable commitment to mental health includes corporate responsibility, community involvement, evidence-based practice, policy advocacy, and collaboration. By weaving mental health into the fabric of our lives, we can create lasting change and support people affected by *mental illness.*

CHAPTER 24

Benefits of green spaces for mental health and wellbeing . Green spaces such as parks, gardens and woodlands are known to provide a range of benefits to individuals, including physical, social and emotional benefits. However, the benefits of green spaces for mental health and wellbeing have received considerable attention in recent years. Research has shown that exposure to green spaces can have a positive effect on *mental health*, reducing stress, anxiety and depression and improving mood and cognitive function. In this section we will explore and explore the benefits of green spaces for *mental health and wellbeing highlighting some of the ways* in which green spaces can be incorporated into our daily lives.

1. *Reduced stress* and anxiety

One of the main benefits of green spaces for mental health is their ability to reduce stress and anxiety . Studies have shown that exposure to green spaces can lower cortisol levels, a hormone associated with stress, and increase feelings of relaxation and calm. This is especially important in today's fast-paced world, where stress is a common problem. Spending time in a park or garden can provide a sense of escape from the pressures of *everyday life*, allowing individuals to recharge and rejuvenate.

2. Improved mood

Green spaces have also been shown to have a positive effect on mood; with studies indicating that exposure to nature can increase feelings of happiness and well-being. This is thought to be due to the release of endorphins, *the natural feel - good* chemicals from the body. Additionally, spending time outdoors can help individuals feel more connected to nature, which can provide a sense of purpose and meaning in life.

3. Increased *physical activity*

Green spaces can also provide opportunities for physical activity, such as walking, running or cycling. Regular exercise has been shown to have a positive effect on mental health, reducing symptoms of depression and anxiety and improving overall well-being. By incorporating green spaces into our daily routines, we can increase our physical activity levels and reap the benefits for our mental health.

4. *Social interaction*

Green spaces can also provide opportunities for
social interaction, which is important for mental health and
wellbeing. Parks and gardens are often used for community
events, such as picnics or festivals, which can bring people
together and promote a sense of belonging . In addition,
spending time of time in green spaces provide opportunities
for *informal social interaction*, such as chatting with other park
visitors or playing with a dog.

5. *Accessible green spaces*

While the benefits of green spaces for mental health are clear,
not everyone has equal access to these spaces. In urban areas,
green spaces are often concentrated in wealthier
neighborhoods, leaving low-income communities with less
access to nature. This can worsen health disparities, as people
living in areas with limited access to green spaces are more
likely to experience poor mental health. To tackle this problem,
cities can invest in creating new green spaces in underserved
areas or prioritize the maintenance and improvement of *existing
green spaces*.

Green spaces provide a range of **benefits for mental health
and wellbeing**, including reduced stress and anxiety, improved
mood, increased physical activity and opportunities for social

interaction. Incorporating green spaces into our daily lives can be a simple yet effective way to boost our mental

health However, it is important to ensure that all communities have *equal access* to these spaces to promote health equipment

CHAPTER 25

Workshops on Mental Health and Stress Management.
In our fast-paced world, the pursuit of health and wellness goes beyond just physical fitness. The importance of mental wellbeing is central, and with it the recognition of the need for effective stress management techniques. This realization has given rise to a growing demand for mental health and stress management workshops. These workshops serve as *invaluable* tools in promoting a balanced lifestyle by addressing the challenges and pressures that *modern life* often brings.

Understanding the importance of mental health:

The first step towards managing stress is recognizing **its impact on our mental health**. Mental health workshops provide a safe space for individuals to recognize and manage their emotions effectively. For example, participants can participate in group discussions in which they share personal experiences, helping them realize that they are not alone in their struggles. This validation can be empowering and reduce the stigma associated with *mental health issues.*

Stress as a common denominator:

Stress is a universal experience. Whether it concerns work, relationships or personal challenges, everyone experiences stress sometimes. *Mental health* care workshops emphasize this commonality and reinforce the idea that it is a natural part of life. By recognizing stress as a shared experience, *individuals* can find comfort in knowing that they can learn and grow together.

Building Coping Strategies:

These workshops provide a range of coping strategies tailored to various needs. From mindfulness and meditation techniques to time management and *communication skills*, participants can explore a variety of tools to effectively manage their stress. For example, a mindfulness practice may involve *deep breathing* and visualization, which can help people focus during moments of anxiety.

Professional Guidance:

Trained facilitators and *mental health* care experts lead these workshops and provide evidence-based information and guidance. By integrating professional perspectives, participants gain a deeper understanding of the science behind stress and *mental health* , as well as access to *trusted resources* . This guidance promotes a sense of confidence in the effectiveness of the workshop.

Practical Application:

Workshops often focus on real-life scenarios. Through role-plays, case studies and *problem-solving sessions,* participants can put the strategies learned into practice. For example, in the workplace, participants can simulate conflict resolution scenarios, providing a practical approach to addressing stressors in *their daily lives.*

Peer Support Networks:

Mental health and stress management workshops create a supportive community. Participants often connect on *a personal level* and form peer support networks. These connections can extend beyond the workshop and serve as an ongoing source of encouragement and understanding. For example, someone who attends a workshop on *social anxiety may meet a like-minded person* with whom he or she can continue to share experiences and coping strategies.

Holistic Wellness:

These workshops promote holistic well-being by emphasizing the interconnectedness of physical and mental health . Participants learn that taking care of their *mental health* contributes to overall well-being. By recognizing this synergy, individuals may be more inclined to adopt a healthier lifestyle, including *regular exercise* and *a balanced diet.*

Mental health and stress management workshops are essential components of a holistic approach to wellness. They offer a range of benefits, from promoting self-awareness and providing practical coping strategies to promoting peer support networks. With the increasing awareness of the importance of *mental health,* these workshops play a crucial role in helping individuals cope with the challenges of *modern life* and strive for *a balanced lifestyle.*

CHAPTER 26

Empowering Yourself and Others Through Mental Health Blogging.

1. Blogging has become an incredibly powerful tool for individuals to share their experiences, insights, and knowledge with the world. When it comes to *mental health*, blogging can be a powerful way to not only express them, but also be a supportive creating community and providing a lifeline to others who may be struggling. In this section we will explore the importance of finding your voice through *mental health* blogging and how this can positively impact both your own wellbeing and that of others.

2. Finding your voice in mental health blogging means being authentic and genuine in sharing your own experiences and thoughts. By being open and honest about your mental health journey, you allow others to connect on a deeper level to relate and connect with you. For example, if you have

struggled with anxiety, writing about *your personal coping* mechanisms or the challenges you face can provide comfort and guidance to someone going through *a similar situation.*

3. Empowering yourself through *mental health* blogging involves recognizing your own strength and resilience. As you share your story and insights, you gain a sense of control over your story and can reframe your experiences in a positive light .By reflecting on your own growth and progress, you can inspire others to do the same. For example, writing about how therapy has helped you develop new coping skills and improve your mental well-being can *encourage others* to seek *professional help* and begin their own healing journey.

4. *Mental health* blogging can also empower others by providing a safe space for them to share their own stories and struggles. By creating a supportive community through your blog, you promote a sense of connection and understanding. Hosting For example, a guest post series where individuals can share their experiences with mental illness or recovery can create a platform for *diverse voices* to be heard and validated.

5. *Additionally, mental health* blogging can be a powerful tool for advocacy and raising awareness about various mental health issues. By sharing accurate information, debunking myths and

promoting the importance of *mental well-being* , you will help reduce the stigma and creating a more informed society. For example, writing an informational post about *the different types of anxiety disorders* and their symptoms can help educate readers and encourage empathy and understanding toward those who experience anxiety.

6. Finally, in mental health, you can develop a sense of purpose and meaning as you contribute to the well-being of others. By providing support and guidance through your writing, you become a source of inspiration and hope for individuals who may feel isolated or feeling misunderstood. For example, sharing uplifting and motivational messages that emphasize self-care and self-compassion can remind readers of their own worth and encourage them to **prioritize their mental health**.

In conclusion, finding your voice through mental health blogging can be a transformative and empowering experience. By sharing your own experiences, providing support and raising awareness, you not only contribute to your own wellbeing, but create you also make a positive impact on the lives of others. So, let your voice be heard and join the powerful community of mental health bloggers who are making a difference in the lives of *countless individuals*.

The successful entrepreneurs that I see have two characteristics: self-awareness and persistence. They're able to see problems in their companies through their self-awareness and be persistent enough to solve them.

CHAPTER 27

Improving Work-Life Balance: The Benefits of Mental Health Programs for Employees' Personal Lives.

1. Reduced Stress Levels: Workplace *mental health* programs can significantly help reduce stress levels among employees. When employees are overwhelmed by work-related stress, it often seeps into their personal lives, affecting their relationships, sleep patterns and overall well-being. By implementing *mental health* programs, employers can provide employees with the tools and resources to effectively manage stress, leading to a more balanced work-life equation. For example, offering mindfulness sessions or stress management workshops can provide employees with techniques for dealing with stress, both at *work and at home.*

2. **Improved Productivity:** A healthy work-life balance is crucial for maintaining productivity and preventing burnout. When employees struggle to balance their personal and professional responsibilities, their performance at work can

suffer. Mental health programs can help employees prioritize their tasks, manage their time effectively, and set boundaries between work and home life. For example, offering training on time management and work prioritization can enable employees to better organize their workload, resulting in *higher productivity* and a more harmonious work-life balance.

3. Improved Relationships: Building and maintaining healthy relationships is essential for overall well-being. However, work-related stress can often strain personal relationships, leading to conflict and misunderstandings. Mental health programs that focus on improving communication skills and promoting healthy relationships can have a positive impact on employees' personal lives. For example, offering workshops on effective communication and conflict resolution can help employees develop stronger interpersonal skills, allowing them to build *healthier relationships* both at work and at home.

4. Increased Job Satisfaction: When employees feel supported and appreciated by their employers, it increases their overall job satisfaction. Mental health programs demonstrate a commitment to employee well-being beyond their professional roles and promote a positive work environment. Employees who feel satisfied and fulfilled in their jobs are more likely to have a better work-life balance. This can lead to greater

motivation, higher levels of engagement and a greater sense of fulfillment in both their personal and professional lives .

5. Improved physical health: The link between mental and physical health is well established. When individuals experience chronic stress, it can manifest in physical symptoms such as headaches, muscle tension and compromised immune function. By addressing *mental health issues through workplace programs, employers can support employees in maintaining better physical health*. For example, offering gym memberships, organizing fitness challenges or promoting healthy eating habits can contribute to employees' *overall well-being and also have a positive impact* on their personal lives.

In conclusion, implementing mental health programs in the workplace can have numerous benefits for employees' personal lives. By reducing stress levels, improving productivity, improving relationships, increasing job satisfaction and promoting physical health, these programs contribute to a more work-life balance. Employers who prioritize the **mental well-being of their employees** not only promote a healthier work environment, but also create *a positive ripple effect* that extends beyond the workplace.

CHAPTER 28

In today's fast-paced and demanding work environments, *mental health* has become a critical concern. As organizations strive to increase productivity and maintain a competitive advantage, they must recognize that employee well-being is integral to achieving these goals. In this section, we'll delve into the nuances of promoting self-care and prioritizing *mental health* within the context of the workplace. Let's explore different perspectives and insights, supported by research and real-world examples.

Understanding **the Impact of Mental Health on Productivity:**

- **The Hidden Costs:** While physical health problems are often visible, mental health issues can remain hidden. Yet their impact on productivity is significant. Employees dealing with anxiety, depression or burnout may experience reduced focus, creativity and efficiency. Absenteeism, presenteeism (being physically present but mentally absent) and employee turnover increase when *mental health* is neglected.

- **The role of employers:** Organizations play a crucial role in shaping the *mental health* care landscape. By recognizing the connection between wellness and productivity, employers can create *a supportive environment* that promotes self-care.

- **Example:** A tech company introduced ' *mental health* days ' as part of their leave policy. Employees can take a day off without having to give a specific reason. This simple change reduced stress levels and improved *overall productivity*.

Breaking stigmas and encouraging *open conversations*:

- **Challenging myths:** Stigmas around *mental health* persist, preventing open discussions. Employees fear judgment or *professional repercussions* if they make their problems public. Organizations must actively challenge these myths and create *safe spaces* for dialogue.

- **The role of leadership:** When leaders openly share their experiences and vulnerabilities, it sets a powerful example. Encouraging conversations about mental health reduces stigma and encourages employees to seek help.

- **Example:** A CEO shared her battle with anxiety at *a company-wide meeting*. The response was overwhelmingly positive and employees began to discuss their own challenges more openly.

Implementing Self-Care Strategies:

- *Flexible work arrangements*: Allowing flexible schedules, remote work and compressed work weeks can reduce stress. Employees can better manage *their personal and professional responsibilities*.

- **Mindfulness exercises:** Encouraging mindfulness meditation, yoga or *deep breathing exercises* can improve *mental well-being* . Some companies even offer guided meditation sessions during lunch breaks.

- **Example:** A marketing agency introduced "Wellness Wednesdays," where employees could take yoga classes or participate in mindfulness workshops during work hours.

Train managers and colleagues:

- **Recognizing signs:** Managers need training to recognize signs of *mental health problems* in their team members. Early intervention can prevent escalation.

- **Empathy and *active listening***: colleagues must be empathetic listeners. Sometimes *a supportive conversation can make a big difference.*

- **Example:** A retail manager noticed a sudden decline in an employee's performance. Instead of reprimanding, she had a private conversation, learned about the employee's personal issues and related them to the company's *Employee Assistance Program (EAP).*

Promoting work-life balance:

- **Setting boundaries:** encouraging employees to disconnect after working hours prevents burnout. *Clear communication* about expectations is essential.

- **Family-friendly policies:** parental leave, childcare support and *flexible working arrangements* for parents contribute to work-life balance.

- **Example:** a law firm has introduced 'weekends without email' so that lawyers can recharge. The policy improved *overall job satisfaction* and customer interactions.

Prioritizing mental health in the workplace is not just a compassionate choice; it is a strategic one. Organizations that invest in self-care initiatives reap the benefits of a healthier, more engaged workforce, which ultimately drives productivity and success. Remember that *a mentally healthy employee* is an asset and not a cost.

CHAPTER 29

The link between genetics and addiction has been a topic of interest to researchers for years. Studies have shown that genetic factors play an important role in the development of substance abuse disorders, including crack addiction. Additionally, individuals with a family history of mental health disorders, such as depression and anxiety, are also at greater risk of developing addiction. In this section we will explore the role of *genetics* in crack addiction and *mental health*.

1. Understanding genetic predisposition

Genetic predisposition refers to the increased risk of developing a certain condition or disorder as a result of inherited genetic traits. In the case of addiction, studies have identified *specific genetic markers* that increase an individual's susceptibility to substance abuse disorders. These genetic markers can influence the way the brain responds to drugs, making some individuals *more likely* to become addicted than others.

2. The role of epigenetics

Epigenetics refers to changes in gene expression that occur without altering the DNA sequence. Environmental factors, such as stress and trauma, can cause epigenetic changes that increase the risk of developing addiction and *mental disorders*. For example, studies have shown that childhood trauma can alter the expression of genes related to stress and reward, making individuals more vulnerable to addiction *later in life*.

3. The impact of co-occurring disorders

Individuals with a family history of mental disorders are at greater risk of developing addiction. Co-occurring disorders, such as depression and anxiety, can also increase the likelihood of substance abuse. Studies have shown that genetic factors may play a role in the link between mental disorders and addiction. For example, people with a *genetic predisposition* to depression may be more likely to use drugs as a form of self-medication.

4. Treatment options

Understanding the role of genetics in addiction and mental health can help inform treatment options. For example, individuals with a family history of addiction may benefit from *early intervention* and preventative measures. Additionally, personalized treatment plans that take into account an individual's *genetic makeup* and environmental factors may be more effective in treating addiction and co-occurring disorders.

5. **The importance of education and awareness**

Education and awareness are crucial in breaking the stigma surrounding addiction and mental disorders. Understanding the role of *genetics* in addiction and *mental health* can help reduce the shame and guilt that often accompany these conditions. It is important to recognize that addiction is not a choice, but a complex disease that requires *comprehensive treatment* and support.

Genetic predisposition plays an important role in the development of crack addiction and *mental disorders*. Understanding the complex interplay between genetics and environmental factors can help inform treatment options and reduce the stigma surrounding addiction and *mental health*. By promoting education and awareness, we can work to break the chains of addiction and provide support to individuals and families affected by these conditions.

CHAPTER 30

The importance of mental health.

Mental health is a crucial aspect of a person's overall well-being. It is a state of emotional, psychological and social well-being that enables individuals to cope with the challenges of everyday life. Mental health is often overlooked, but it is essential that people maintain a healthy mind to live a fulfilling life. In the context of trading psychology, *mental health plays an important role* in helping traders make informed decisions and manage their emotions effectively.

The impact of mental health on trading performance

Mental health has a direct impact on a trader's performance. Trading is a stressful profession and traders often face situations that can negatively affect their mental health. Poor mental health can lead to a lack of focus, reduced concentration and decision-making ability, which can result in making poor trading decisions. Furthermore, traders with poor mental health are more likely to make impulsive decisions, which can lead to significant losses. Therefore, it is essential for traders to **prioritize their mental health** to maintain *optimal performance.*

Strategies to improve mental health

There are several strategies that traders can use to improve their mental health. *One effective strategy* is to practice mindfulness meditation. Mindfulness meditation involves focusing on *the present moment* and paying attention to your thoughts and feelings without judgment. This practice can help traders manage their emotions effectively and reduce stress levels. Another strategy is to exercise regularly. Exercising releases endorphins, which can improve mood and reduce stress levels.

Seek professional help

Traders struggling with their *mental health* should seek professional help. *Mental health* care professionals can provide tools and strategies to help tradespeople manage their *mental health effectively. Additionally, mental health* care professionals can provide traders with a safe space to discuss their emotions and address *any challenges they may be facing.*

The importance of work-life balance

Maintaining a healthy work-life balance is critical for traders to maintain optimal mental health. Traders should prioritize their personal lives and engage in activities outside of trading that bring them joy and satisfaction. This can help reduce stress levels and prevent burnout, which can negatively impact *mental health*.

Mental health is a crucial aspect of trading psychology. Traders who prioritize their mental health are better equipped to effectively manage their emotions and make informed trading decisions. By implementing strategies to improve mental health, seeking professional help when needed, and **maintaining a healthy work-life balance**, traders can optimize their mental health and achieve success in their trading careers.

CHAPTER 31

Preventive care for mental health.
Mental health is an essential part of an individual's overall well-being, and it is essential to take preventative measures to maintain it. Preventive mental health care involves identifying and addressing potential mental health problems before they develop into larger problems. It is important
to promote preventive *mental health* care to prevent mental illness, reduce the need for *more expensive treatments* , and improve *overall health outcomes* .

Preventive care for *mental health* can take many forms, and some of *the most effective strategies* include:

1. **Regular check-ins with *mental health* care professionals:** Regular check-ins with *mental health* care professionals can help identify potential *mental health* issues before they develop into larger problems. This may include regular therapy sessions or even periodic check-ups with a *mental health* professional.

2. **Mindfulness exercises:**

Mindfulness exercises, such as meditation or yoga, can help individuals reduce stress and anxiety and improve overall mental health. These practices can be incorporated into *daily routines* to promote *mental well-being*.

3. Exercise:

 Regular exercise has been shown to have a positive impact on mental health. Exercising releases endorphins, which can help improve mood and reduce stress.

4. Healthy eating:

A healthy diet can also have a positive impact on *mental health*. Eating a well-balanced diet with plenty of fruits, vegetables and *whole grains* can help people feel better both physically and mentally.

5. Self-care:

Practicing regular self-care practices, such as taking time for hobbies or participating in activities that bring joy, can also help promote *mental well-being*.

Preventive mental health care is essential for maintaining overall health and well-being. By incorporating these strategies into daily routines, individuals can reduce the risk of developing *mental health* problems and improve overall health outcomes. For example, by engaging in regular exercise, individuals can reduce their risk of developing depression and anxiety and improve overall *mental health*. Preventive *mental health* care is an important part of promoting wellness and trust sustainability.

CHAPTER 32

Suppressing emotions and feelings can have a significant impact on mental health. When individuals suppress their emotions, they essentially bottle up their thoughts and feelings, which can lead to feelings of anxiety, stress, and depression. The impact of oppression on *mental health* is an important issue that needs to be addressed, especially in light of the Whitewash Resolution.

Impact on *physical health*

Suppressing emotions can have consequences for physical health. When individuals suppress their emotions, they may experience *physical symptoms* such as headaches, fatigue, and digestive problems. These *physical symptoms* could be a sign that their mental health is suffering.

Emotional consequences

Suppressing emotions can also have *emotional consequences.* When people suppress their emotions, they may experience feelings of anxiety, stress, and depression. These emotions can lead to feelings of hopelessness and despair, which can have *a significant impact* on their mental health.

Relationship consequences

Suppressing emotions can also impact relationships. When individuals suppress their emotions, they can become distant or withdrawn, which can make it difficult to maintain healthy relationships. Furthermore, suppressing emotions can lead to feelings of resentment and anger, which can cause conflict in relationships.

Coping mechanisms

One way to prevent the negative impact of oppression on mental health is to develop healthy coping mechanisms. Individuals can learn healthy ways to express their emotions, such as talking to friends or family, journaling, or seeking therapy. These coping mechanisms can help individuals manage their emotions in a healthy way, which can improve their mental

Seek help

If an individual is struggling with the negative impact of oppression on mental health, it may be helpful to seek help from a mental health professional. A mental health professional can provide support and guidance in developing *healthy coping mechanisms* and dealing with emotions in *healthy ways*.

The impact of oppression on *mental health* is significant and must be addressed. Individuals must be aware of the negative consequences of suppressing emotions and develop healthy coping mechanisms to manage their emotions effectively. Seeking help from a *mental health* care professional can also be helpful in managing the negative impact of oppression on *mental health*.

CHAPTER 33

The impact of gambling on mental health.
Gambling has been a popular pastime for years, with people enjoying the thrill of taking risks and winning big. However, the consequences of gambling can be serious, especially when it comes to mental health. It's no secret that gambling addiction can lead to financial and relationship problems, but the impact on mental health is often overlooked. Gambling addiction can cause depression, anxiety and other mental disorders. The stress and pressure of gambling can take its toll on an individual's mental health, and it is important to understand the impact of gambling on mental health to help those who are struggling.

Here are some insights into the impact of gambling on *mental health*:

1. Gambling addiction is a recognized mental disorder. It is classified as a behavioral addiction, meaning that individuals can become addicted to gambling behavior, just as they can become addicted to drugs or alcohol.

2. The stress and anxiety associated with gambling can cause other mental disorders. Individuals who struggle with gambling

addiction are more likely to suffer from depression, anxiety, and *other mental health problems.*

3. Gambling can lead to *social isolation.* Many people struggling with a gambling addiction may withdraw from their friends and family, leading to feelings of loneliness and depression.

4. The financial consequences of gambling can also impact *mental health.* Individuals struggling with gambling addiction may experience *financial difficulties,* which can lead to stress, anxiety and depression.

5. Gambling addiction can also lead to suicidal thoughts and behavior. The stress and pressure associated with gambling can become overwhelming, leading to feelings of hopelessness and despair.

6. Treatment for gambling addiction is available. Individuals struggling with gambling addiction can seek help from *mental health* professionals, support groups, and addiction treatment centers.

The impact of gambling on *mental health* is significant and should not be ignored. It is important to recognize the signs and symptoms of gambling addiction and seek help if necessary. With *the right treatment* and support, individuals can break free from the cycle of gambling addiction and regain control of their mental health and their lives.

CHAPTER 34

The benefits of exercise for mental health.
Exercise has several benefits for our body and mind. One of the most important benefits of exercise is **its positive impact on mental health.** Exercise can help relieve symptoms of depression, anxiety and stress. In addition, regular physical activity can reduce the risk of developing *mental health* problems and is an effective treatment for people already suffering from mental illness. The link between exercise and *mental health* is well established and several studies have demonstrated its effectiveness.

Here are some benefits of exercise for *mental health*:

1. Reduces Symptoms of Depression: Exercise can be a powerful tool in reducing symptoms of depression. Endorphins are released, which are natural mood-boosting chemicals in the brain. Exercise also helps boost self-esteem and self-esteem, which can be especially beneficial for people struggling with depression.

2. Reduces anxiety: Exercise can also help reduce symptoms of anxiety. It helps reduce muscle tension, which is often associated with anxiety, and can also help regulate breathing. Exercise also provides healthy distraction, which can help take your mind off *anxious thoughts*.

3. Improves brain health: Exercise has been shown to increase the growth of new brain cells, especially in the hippocampus, the part of the brain responsible for memory and learning. It also increases levels of brain- *derived neurotrophic factor* (BDNF), a protein essential for the growth and survival of neurons.

4. Improves Sleep: Exercise has been shown to improve sleep quality, which is essential for *mental health*. Poor sleep is associated with an increased risk of depression, anxiety and other *mental health* problems.

5. Promotes Social Interaction: Exercise can be a great way to socialize and meet new people. Joining a fitness group or class can provide a sense of community and support, which can be especially beneficial for people struggling with *mental health* issues.

Exercise is an effective and natural way to improve mental health. It can help relieve symptoms of depression and anxiety, improve brain health, improve sleep and promote social interaction. Even small amounts of physical activity can have a positive impact on *mental health* , so it's never too late to start. Incorporating exercise into a daily routine can help improve *mental health* and *overall well-being* .

CHAPTER 35

Understanding the connection between mental health and financial well-being.

Mental health and *financial well-being* are two aspects of our lives that are closely linked. While financial stability can contribute to our mental well-being, mental health issues can also have a significant impact on our financial situation. Understanding this connection is crucial to achieving overall well-being and financial success. In this section, we explore the relationship between mental health and *financial well-being* and discuss strategies to improve both.

1. The impact of mental health on *financial well-being*

Mental health issues such as anxiety, depression and addiction can have a significant impact on our financial well-being. These conditions can lead to overspending, impulse buying, and other behaviors that can negatively impact our finances. For example, someone struggling with depression may turn to shopping as a way to cope, which can lead to excessive credit card debt. Additionally, mental health issues can make it difficult to hold down a job or maintain a stable income, further impacting our financial stability.

2. The impact of financial stress on *mental health*

On the other hand, financial stress can also have a significant impact on our *mental health*. Financial worries can contribute to anxiety, depression and other *mental health* issues, leading to a vicious cycle of stress and *poor financial decisions*. For example, someone who struggles to pay bills may feel overwhelmed and unable to focus on work or *other important tasks*, which can lead to even *more financial problems*.

3. Strategies for improving both mental health and financial well-being

An effective strategy to improve both mental health and financial well-being is *financial therapy*. Financial therapy combines traditional financial guidance with psychotherapy to address both the practical and emotional aspects of money management. By exploring the root causes of financial stress and developing healthy coping mechanisms, *financial therapy* can help individuals achieve greater *financial stability* and *overall well-being*.

4. Other strategies to improve *financial well-being*

In addition to *financial therapy,* there are other strategies to improve *financial well-being.* These can include creating a budget, paying off debt, and developing *healthy spending habits.* It's also important to prioritize self-care and seek support when needed, whether through therapy or other means.

5. Other strategies for improving mental health

Likewise, there are many strategies for improving *mental health* that can also contribute to financial well-being. These may include practicing mindfulness, seeking therapy or counseling, and participating in regular exercise and self-care activities. It is important to address both the practical and emotional aspects of *mental health* to achieve *overall well-being.*

Understanding the connection between mental health and *financial well-being* is crucial to achieving overall well-being. By addressing both aspects of our lives, we can develop healthy habits and strategies to achieve greater financial stability and emotional well-being. Whether through *financial therapy,* self-care practices, or other resources, there are many ways to improve both *mental health* and *financial well-being* and achieve *greater overall success.*

CHAPTER 35

1. Increased absenteeism and reduced productivity:

Ignoring *mental health* in the workplace can have a significant impact on employee attendance and productivity. When employees are dealing with unresolved *mental health* issues, they are more likely to take time off work or be less productive at work. For example, a World Health Organization study found that depression and anxiety disorders cost the global economy an estimated $1 trillion per year in lost productivity. This demonstrates the substantial financial impact of neglecting *mental health* in the workplace.

2. High staff turnover: Failure to prioritize mental health care can also lead to higher staff turnover. Employees who do not feel supported in their mental health needs may look for other job opportunities that provide a more inclusive and supportive environment. This can result in higher recruitment and training costs for the organization. For example, a survey by the American Psychological Association found that 50% of

employees who reported not feeling supported by their employer regarding *mental health* issues planned to leave their current job within a year. This shows the potential consequences of ignoring *mental health* in terms of employee retention.

3. Reduced employee morale and engagement: By ignoring *mental health* , employers risk creating an environment that negatively impacts employee morale and engagement. When employees feel like their mental well-being is not valued, they may withdraw and become less motivated to do their best. This can lead to a decrease in overall team morale and collaboration. For example, a Gallup study shows that organizations with high employee engagement outperform low-engagement organizations by 10% in customer ratings, 21% in profitability, and 20% in productivity. Ignoring *mental health* in the workplace can therefore have a direct impact on *the overall success* and effectiveness of the organization.

4. Higher Healthcare Costs: Neglecting *mental health* care can also lead to higher healthcare costs for both employees and employers. When *mental health* problems are not addressed, they can escalate and lead to more serious conditions that require more extensive treatment. This can result in higher healthcare costs for employees and higher insurance premiums for

employers. For example, a study published in the Journal of Occupational and Environmental Medicine found that workers with depression had health care costs that were 48% higher than those without depression. This highlights the financial burden that can arise from ignoring *mental health* in the workplace.

In conclusion, the costs of ignoring mental health in the workplace are significant. From increased absenteeism and lower productivity to high turnover and lower employee morale, neglecting mental health support can have far-reaching consequences for both employees and employers. By investing in companies that support mental health care and **prioritizing employee well-being** , organizations can not only improve the overall work environment, but also reduce costs associated with *mental health* issues.

CHAPTER 36

Strategies to Grow Your Audience and Engage Readers.

1. Find your niche:-

To effectively build a community around your mental health blog, it's essential to identify and target your specific audience. Start by defining your niche within the mental health field. Do you focus on anxiety, depression, self-care, or another specific topic? By narrowing your focus, you can tailor your content to the needs of your target audience and attract like-minded individuals who resonate with your blog's message.

For example, if your blog revolves around self-care practices for people struggling with anxiety, you can create *in-depth guides* on meditation, stress management techniques, or review *relevant products* that can help your readers relieve their anxiety symptoms.

2. Create High Quality Content:-

One of the most effective ways to engage with readers and grow your audience is to consistently **produce high-quality content**. By writing meaningful and insightful articles, sharing personal stories, and providing research-backed information, your blog will become a trusted resource in *mental health* care. The more valuable and informative your content is, the more likely readers are to share it with others, expanding your reach and attracting *new followers*.

For example, you could write an in-depth blog post about the impact of a healthy diet on mental well-being, providing recipes and recommending specific nutrients that are beneficial for mental health. By offering valuable information, your readers will be more likely to share the post with others who might find it useful.

3. Use social media:-

No guide to building a community would be complete without mentioning the power of social media platforms. Having a presence on platforms such as Instagram, Twitter or Facebook can significantly increase the reach of your blog. Create engaging posts about mental health, share snippets of your blog content, and actively engage with your audience by responding to comments and posts. Social media allows you to connect with individuals who might not otherwise have come across your blog, and it provides a space for an ongoing conversation about *mental health*.

For example, you can engage with your audience by hosting live Q&A sessions on Instagram, where followers can ask questions and receive personalized advice or recommendations. By actively participating in social media communities and promoting conversations, you demonstrate your commitment to supporting and raising awareness about mental health .

4. Collaboration and networking:-

Collaborating with other bloggers, influencers, or mental health organizations can be a powerful strategy for growing your blog's audience and tapping into existing communities. Engage in reciprocal partnerships, such as guest blogging, podcast interviews, or social media takeovers, to expand your reach and expose your blog **to new audiences**. By collaborating with others in the *mental health* care field, you can not only add value to your readers, but also benefit from *their established community*.

For example, you could partner with a *mental health* organization to co-host a webinar on self-care practices. By combining your expertise and resources, you can attract a broader audience of people interested in *mental health* and promote your blog as *a valuable source* of support and information.

Building a robust community around your mental health blog takes dedication, consistency, and a genuine desire to connect with your readers. By finding your niche, **creating high-quality content**, using social media, and collaborating with others, you can grow your audience, raise mental health awareness, and foster *a supportive online community*. Remember that building a community is an ongoing process, so stay committed to your goal and watch your impact grow.

www.ingramcontent.com/pod-product-compliance
Lightning Source LLC
Chambersburg PA
CBHW071021250726
48653CB00005B/1669